SECRETS OF THE UNEXPLAINED

Alien Astronauts

by Gary L. Blackwood

BENCHMARK BOOKS

MARSHALL CAVENDISH
NEW YORK

Benchmark Books
Marshall Cavendish Corporation
99 White Plains Road
Tarrytown, New York 10591

Library of Congress Cataloging-in-Publication Data
Blackwood, Gary L.
Alien astronauts / Gary L. Blackwood.
p.   cm. — (Secrets of the unexplained)
Includes index.
Summary: discusses the existence of unidentified flying objects and
explanations for various sightings throughout history.
ISBN 0-7614-0469-4 (lib. bdg.)
1. Unidentified flying objects—Juvenile literature. [1. Unidentified flying objects.]
I. Title. II. Series: Blackwood, Gary L. Secrets of the unexplained.
TL789.2.B53   1999   001.942—dc21   97-13 CIP   AC

Printed in Hong Kong

Photo Credits
Front cover: courtesy of Charles Walker Collection/Stock Montage; front cover inset: courtesy of Debbie
Lee/Fortean Picture Library; back cover: courtesy of Jeremy Johnson/Fortean Picture Library; page 6: Woody
Akins/Fortean Picture Library; pages 8-9: D. Carroll/ The Image Bank; page 10: Charles Walker
Collection/Stock Montage; page 11: Werner Forman/Art Resource, NY; page 13: Scala/Art Resource, NY; pages
16, 17, 21: Mary Evans Picture Library, London; pages 20, 47, 57, 61: Fortean Picture Library; page 22:
George Adamski/Fortean Picture Library; page 25: Llewellyn Publications/Fortean Picture Library; page 26:
Paul Villa/Fortean Picture Library; page 29: Columbia (Courtesy Kobal); pages 30, 31: Paul Trent/Mary Evans
Picture Library, London; pages 32, 58: Peregrine Mendoza/Fortean Picture Library; pages 34-35: Amilton
Vieira/Fortean Picture Library; page 36: Jeremy Johnson/Fortean Picture Library; pages 38, 39: Hessdalen
Project/Mary Evans Picture Library, London; pages 40-41: Ella Louise Fortune/Mary Evans Picture Library,
London; page 42: Anges Sanborn/Charles Walker Collection/Stock Montage; page 51: Philip Daly/Charles
Walker Collection/Stock Montage; page 53: Terence Meaden/Mary Evans Picture Library, London; page 65:
Werner Burger/Fortean Picture Library; page 67: United States Air Force; pages 70-71: James Crocker/Fortean
Picture Library

1   3   5   6   4   2

Contents

Introduction

It was almost dark when Monsieur Belans saw the strange craft. He'd been strolling through the countryside of Belgium, in an area where farmers had recently noticed odd flattened places in their crops, as if something large and heavy had lain there. Ahead of him Belans saw a man dressed in black standing under a tree, obviously waiting for someone—or something. Belans soon found out what.

He heard a buzzing sound overhead, then a brightly lighted oval craft swooped down and landed near him. Instead of feeling fear or alarm, Belans just felt tired, as if something had drained all his energy.

A door opened in the strange craft, and the man in black climbed in. Belans felt compelled to follow. He found himself in a room that was bright but had no light fixtures that he could see. The door closed, and the craft rose into the air.

A tall man entered the room. He seemed to be able to read Belans's thoughts. In perfect French, he said that he came from a distant star and that he and his fellow aliens were being careful not to be seen by many people, for fear of upsetting the "natural order of things" on Earth.

Eventually, Belans was returned home safe and sound, but with a long span of time unaccounted for.

Most UFO sightings happen at night, and the witness doesn't see an actual spacecraft, just a bright light.

What do you make of Belans's strange encounter? Was it:

A) a hallucination? Was Belans just seeing things?

B) a real event? Did he actually take a ride in an alien spaceship?

C) an unexplainable occurrence, maybe real, maybe not?

D) a science fiction story?

If you picked A, you're a skeptic. You figure there must be a logical, rational explanation. You're in good company. A recent Gallup poll says that 30 percent of Americans think that UFOs—Unidentified Flying Objects—are purely imaginary.

If you chose B, you're a believer. You feel sure that there must be intelligent life out there somewhere and that it's checking up on us. You have even more people on your side. According to that same poll, 49 percent of us are convinced that UFOs are real.

If you went with C, you're just not sure—like 21 percent of Americans.

If you said D . . . you're absolutely right. Surprised? What's even more surprising is that the story wasn't written in the 1990s, or even in the 1950s, when stories of "flying saucers" filled magazines and newspapers. The story of Monsieur Belans was written in 1930, long before anyone had heard of crop circles or alien abductions.

PART ONE

The Long, Strange History of Alien Encounters

The colorful globes that floated over Basel, Switzerland, on August 7, 1566, seemed to emerge from several cylinder-shaped "mother ships."

Shields, Ships, and Saucers

Obviously UFOs aren't just a modern phenomenon. In fact, people have been seeing strange things in the skies for as long as history has been recorded—and even before that. Dozens of cultures around the world have myths about visitors from space who give us Earthlings some new bits of wisdom or information.

Australian aborigines believe the world was created by the *wondinja*, spirits who came to Earth in flying craft and who left behind pictures of themselves on trees and cave walls. A Native American legend says that a red-eyed man with great healing powers once lived

The myths of the Dogon people of Africa are depicted in their cave paintings. One says that beings from "the land of the fish"—the Sirius star system—visited Earth long ago in a great ark that shot flames and that they will return.

among the Yakima tribe; when the stranger died, an object descended from the sky and took away his body. According to another Native American tradition, spirits called kachinas came from other planets to teach the Hopi tribe how to farm and how to behave properly.

The Dogon people of Africa have long known scientific facts about the Sirius star system—facts that seemingly could have come only from a much more advanced civilization. They claim that the knowledge was brought to them from Sirius itself, by amphibious creatures called the Nommo.

But we have more than just legends to draw on. Written accounts of flying saucers and alien visitors go back to at least the fourth century, when citizens of Rome saw circular "shields" and burning globes in the sky. In the eighth century, Saxons laying siege to the town of Sigiburg in Germany fled in panic when what appeared to be two huge red shields rose above the church.

In ninth-century France, farmers were very disturbed by "cloud-ships" that kept ruining their crops. They suspected three men and a woman of being passengers from the aerial vessels, and stoned them to death.

The first recorded military investigation of a UFO took place in 1235, when a Japanese general saw lights circling in the sky and ordered his aides to study them. They concluded that the lights were the result of the "wind making the stars sway."

In 1561 the skies over Nuremberg, Germany, were filled with strange cylinders, which released colored spheres that zoomed about, trailing smoke. Five years later the residents of Basel, Switzerland, were treated to a similar display.

Unidentified aerial objects aren't just a modern phenomenon. With a magnifying glass, check out the strange shape in the upper right of this fifteenth-century painting by Domenico Ghirlandaio.

Edmond Halley, the British astronomer who charted Halley's comet, wrote that in 1716 glowing shapes lit up the night sky so brightly that he could read a book by the light.

A sighting by a Texas farmer in 1878 wasn't especially notable except for one thing: The farmer described the dark shape that passed over him as a "large saucer." This was the first time a witness had used that term, but far from the last.

Cigars and Mars

Those early witnesses described the unfamiliar objects in terms that were familiar to them: shields, ships, saucers. When the first major wave of sightings hit the United States in 1897, newspapers dubbed the UFOs "mystery airships." Most witnesses described the craft as cigar-shaped, with a lighted basket slung underneath, much like the dirigibles that were developed a few years later. But no dirigible was capable of the kinds of maneuvers performed by these airships. They flew into the wind at unheard-of speeds and could rise abruptly straight into the air.

In cities across the country, the streets at night were filled with people staring into the skies, hoping for a glimpse of the objects. Meanwhile, in rural areas, a few people were having close encounters with the airships and their occupants. Nearly always the visitors were not strange-looking aliens, but ordinary humans who wanted food or water, or tools to fix their craft.

Several inventors claimed credit for the airships and promised to unveil their inventions publicly, but none ever did. When the famous inventor Thomas Edison declared that the airships were undoubtedly a hoax, interest in them dwindled, and so did the number of reports of flying objects.

But they didn't go away. In June 1908 one literally exploded on the scene. A huge, shiny cylinder streaked across the sky over Siberia, changed direction, then blew up three miles above the surface of the earth, with a force ten times that of the Hiroshima bomb. The blast flattened trees four hundred miles away and registered on seismographs all around the world. For several nights the sky over northern Europe glowed brightly from the huge clouds of dust thrown up by the blast. It's unlikely that the cause of the explosion was a meteorite, since meteorites don't change course. The evidence suggests some kind of nuclear explosion—forty years before the atomic bomb was developed.

In 1909 the cigar shapes reappeared and were sighted for the next fourteen years, not just in America but also in Japan, New Zealand, and Europe. When a strange craft drifted over the naval yards at Kent, England, in 1912, Winston Churchill, then First Lord of the Admiralty, brought the subject up before Parliament. It was the first time a politician had publicly admitted that there were unidentified objects in the skies.

In the period between the two world wars, the skies were relatively quiet. Then, in February 1942, two months after the Japanese attack on Pearl Harbor brought the United States into World War II, a large, dark object floated over Los Angeles. Nervous antiaircraft gunners opened fire on it, with no effect. This was definitely not another Japanese attack. In August twenty more objects zoomed over Los Angeles while gun crews blazed away at them.

World War II pilots regularly spotted "foo fighters"—bright lights that darted about as if playing tag with the airplanes. The term "foo" is probably a variation of the French word feu, *meaning "fire."*

During the war fighter pilots on both sides came back from their missions with tales of balls of light that chased their airplanes. American pilots called the lights "foo fighters," after the 1940s comic-strip character Smokey Stover, whose favorite line was "Where there's foo, there's fire." The pilots were worried that the lights might be a secret weapon developed by the Germans. Meanwhile, the German fighter pilots were convinced that the fast-moving balls of light were an American invention.

Shortly after the war, in 1946, more than a thousand rocketlike shapes called "ghost rockets" were sighted over Scandinavia. The Swedish military suspected they were Russian weapons, but there's no evidence that the Soviet Union, or any other country, was testing rockets over Europe, and certainly not by the thousands.

In a world racked by war, it was natural for people to see strange aerial objects as enemy weapons. But scientists offered lots of other

Soon after World War II ended, cigar-shaped objects were repeatedly seen over Scandinavia and Western Europe. United States Army Intelligence identified 80 percent of the "ghost rockets" as natural phenomena but left the other 20 percent unexplained.

possible explanations: a bright star or planet, a flight of birds, a meteor, a balloon, a cloud formation, or some sort of hoax. Occasionally someone suggested that the current crop of unexplained objects might be alien craft from Mars or from deep inside the earth. But these theories weren't taken very seriously.

So far no one had given much thought to the overall phenomenon of UFOs, and no one had tried to show that the various sightings were somehow related. In the late 1940s all that changed. The objects that people had been calling shields or airships or foo fighters or ghost rockets were suddenly lumped together in a single category: flying saucers.

The Flying Saucer Era

Nineteen forty-seven was a good year for sightings, especially in the northwestern United States. Officially the government dismissed the reports as nonsense. But secretly the Air Force was alarmed and began an investigation called Project Sign. An Air Force report dated July 30 concluded that "this 'flying saucer' situation is not at all imaginary. . . . Something is really flying around."

Obviously the term *flying saucer* was already in wide use. The newspapers had coined it only a month earlier, when they published a story of a private pilot named Kenneth Arnold. On June 24, 1947, Arnold had been searching for a downed plane near Mount Rainier, in Washington State, when he spotted nine bright, crescent-shaped objects sailing over the mountaintops. Using his dashboard clock, he estimated their speed at about seventeen hundred miles per hour. He guessed they were forty-five to fifty feet long. But if Arnold misjudged the distance, the objects could have been slower and smaller. In fact, the drawings he made of the objects suggest that he might have seen a flock of birds reflecting the sun's light. But the reporters

Kenneth Arnold never described the nine daylight discs he saw as being saucer-shaped, but newspaper accounts gave the public that impression.

latched on to his verbal description: "They flew," he said, "like a saucer would if you skipped it across water." Arnold never said the objects *looked* like saucers, but as the story spread across the country, the term *flying saucer* caught the public's fancy.

The Arnold incident set off an avalanche of other reports. Not surprisingly, most of them described the craft they saw as saucer-shaped. For the next ten years America went flying-saucer crazy. The fad was fueled by best-selling books such as Frank Scully's *Behind the Flying Saucers* and Donald Keyhoe's *Flying Saucers from Outer Space*. Hollywood cashed in on the craze by producing movies titled *The Thing, The Red Planet Mars, It Came from Outer Space,* and *The Day the Earth Stood Still*.

People were willing to believe that anything and everything in the sky was a flying saucer. There was a rash of "contactees"—people who claimed to have met the alien pilots of the saucers face-to-face. The

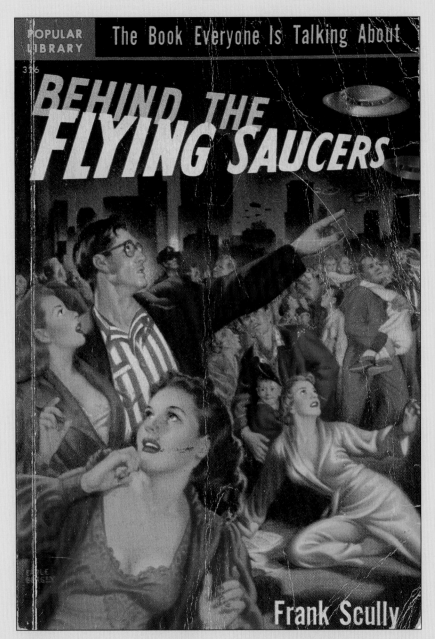

The Book Everyone Is Talking About

326

BEHIND THE FLYING SAUCERS

Frank Scully

Frank Scully's 1950 book Behind the Flying Saucers *claimed that the Air Force had captured three saucers containing sixteen alien bodies. Though many of the book's details proved false, it became a best-seller.*

claims of these Earthlings got more and more outrageous as they tried to top one another.

The most famous contactee was George Adamski, a handyman who insisted he'd been taken aboard spaceships from no fewer than four different planets. The space people, he said, had given him a message of great importance to pass on to other Earthlings: Stop atomic testing.

Another contactee, Howard Menger, claimed that aliens had given him more practical things: a "space potato" with five times the protein of an Earth potato; a "free energy" motor that unfortunately did nothing; and a newfound ability to play the piano.

Astronomer J. Allen Hynek pointed out that Adamski's photo of the aliens' spacecraft bore a close resemblance to a chicken brooder.

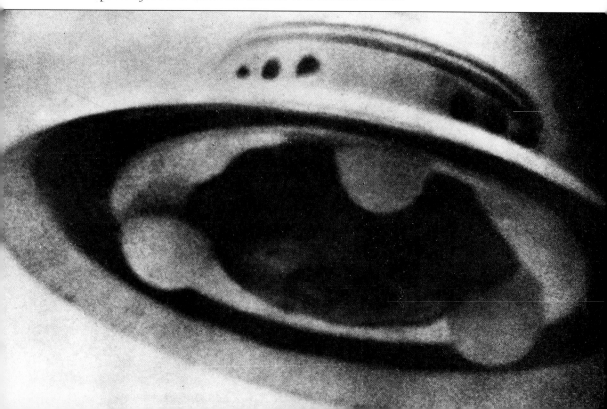

Several of the contactees became celebrities. They published popular books, made regular appearances on TV and radio, and had thousands of loyal followers who were convinced that their stories were true.

How could so many people fall for such outlandish claims? In the 1950s the threat of nuclear destruction hung over the world, so it was comforting to think that some greater intelligence would come along and bail us out. Believers banded together in hundreds of flying-saucer clubs. Before long these groups, whose members were willing to accept nearly anything, made the whole idea of flying saucers seem foolish and anyone who reported seeing them seem loony. Kenneth Arnold, the pilot who had started it all, now declared, "If I saw a ten-story building flying through the air, I would never say a word about it."

In the midst of all this commotion, a few organizations were doing their best to study the problem scientifically. And there were plenty of witnesses who couldn't be dismissed as crackpots. One of them was Clyde Tombaugh, the astronomer who discovered the planet Pluto. Even Britain's Air Chief was convinced that saucers came "from some extraterrestrial source."

The Air Force Investigates

The United States Air Force was getting three thousand letters a month from school kids asking for more information on flying saucers. The military was still trying to make people believe that saucers were an illusion, brought on by something called "Buck Rogers trauma"—a fear of new technology. At the same time the Air Force was continuing its investigation, under the title Project Grudge, later called Project Blue Book. Whatever the name, the purpose of the investigation was always the same: to prove that flying saucers didn't exist.

Air Force investigators did manage to explain away most of the sightings as weather balloons or comets, meteors or stars. But a small percentage had to be classified as "unknowns." The Air Force didn't make public the fact that there were "unknowns" for fear of causing a panic. Frustrated over the cover-up, the head of the project, Edward Ruppelt, resigned. In 1956 he published a book, *The Report on Unidentified Flying Objects*, that told the whole story—and that introduced the term *UFO* as a replacement for *flying saucer*, which now had a bad reputation.

Despite the Air Force's efforts, the UFO controversy didn't go away. Instead it grew, starting with an incident in November 1957: At least twenty witnesses, including police and firefighters, watched a glowing ball rise from a Texas field with a sound like thunder. There was another much publicized encounter by a police officer in New Mexico in 1964 and, a year later, one in Exeter, New Hampshire. That same year astronaut James McDivitt, aboard *Gemini IV*, saw and photographed a strange cylindrical object.

UFOs had become a serious topic again. But not everyone took

By the 1950s flying saucers were impossible to ignore. They turned up in best-selling books, on movie screens, and on the covers of popular magazines.

The Air Force tried to dismiss the UFO problem, but it wouldn't go away. This UFO was photographed near Albuquerque, New Mexico, on June 16, 1963.

them seriously. Shows such as *Star Trek*, *Lost in Space*, and *The Invaders* invaded TV. The mayor of Brewer, Maine, put up a billboard that read: BREWER WELCOMES UFOS. LANDING SITES AVAILABLE.

The public demanded that the Air Force reopen its investigation. It put a team of scientists to work under the direction of Dr. Edward Condon, one of the physicists who had developed the atomic bomb. Condon was an admitted skeptic. Not surprisingly, the report he and his team made in 1969 concluded that UFOs were mostly hoaxes or natural phenomena and didn't deserve any further investigation. It didn't seem to matter that twenty-three of the incidents they'd studied remained unexplained. The Air Force closed the book on the subject of UFOs.

In the early 1970s, in the wake of the Condon Report, the news media talked about UFOs as if they were nothing more than a passing fad, like the Hula Hoop or coonskin caps.

But then, in 1973, it all started again. There was a new wave of sightings in the United States, as big as those of 1897 and 1947. A 1973 Gallup poll showed that an astounding 11 percent of Americans had seen a UFO and that 54 percent of the population believed they were real. Books on UFOs made a comeback. Some were serious, well-researched accounts, like John Fuller's *Incident at Exeter*. Others were uneasy mixtures of fact and fancy, like Erich von Däniken's *Chariots of the Gods?* Since the government was apparently no longer interested, UFO groups and individual investigators took on the job of interviewing witnesses and checking out evidence. Scientists took sides in the "UFO Wars." One side stated that UFOs were an undeniable physical fact. The other insisted that they were nonsense.

That debate still rages. Waves of sightings have come and gone in recent years. In 1981 a million people watched a spiral UFO in the skies over China—probably the most-witnessed sighting to date. Two years later some five thousand New Yorkers saw a huge boomerang shape with flashing lights hovering over the Hudson River valley. From 1989 to 1991 a giant lighted triangle was sighted again and again over eastern Belgium. In 1993 many witnesses saw a tube-shaped object pass over England and crash in an isolated area north of the city of York.

Whatever else UFOs may or may not be, they have certainly become a part of our culture. Beginning with the film *Close Encounters of the Third Kind* in 1977, there's been a constant stream of movies and TV shows on the subject. As a result, we've come to expect UFOs to turn up. Famous people, from William Shatner to John Lennon to Jimmy Carter, have publicly admitted seeing them. Harvard professor Timothy Leary and scientist John Lilly claimed to be in touch with aliens telepathically. The new edition of the *Fire Officer's Guide to Disaster Control* advises firefighters what to do if they encounter a UFO (approach it with a positive attitude, and don't display any weapons).

Several UFO sites have turned into major tourist attractions. Nevada Highway 375, where strange lights appear regularly in the

Aliens are about to land in Steven Spielberg's movie Close Encounters of the Third Kind. *It was one of the few movies to feature extraterrestrials that fit the description given by most real-life witnesses.*

Photographic Proof

If UFOs are real, solid objects, why aren't there any good photographs of them? Actually, there are, though not very many. Lots of witnesses have had cameras close by, but either they were so disturbed by the encounter that they didn't think to shoot pictures, or else they felt physically unable to reach for the camera. This could be an effect of the electrical fields associated with UFOs.

Still, dozens of witnesses have managed to take photos of what they saw. The earliest known picture dates back to 1883, when a Mexican astronomer photographed through his telescope a group of glowing objects crossing the sun.

There's been no shortage of phony photos, however. Publicity seekers have snapped everything from an ordinary button to a ceiling light and tried to pass it off as a UFO. In 1962 an English schoolboy took a photo of five strange shapes that fooled UFO investigators for years. Eventually he admitted they were just blobs painted on a sheet of glass.

In 1967 two brothers in Michigan produced a very convincing Polaroid picture of a saucer. For a long time it was considered genuine and turned up often in books about UFOs. But when the boys grew up, they confessed that the UFO was just a small model hanging from a thread.

With today's methods of analyzing photos by computer, it's much easier to spot a fake. But several snapshots of UFOs have managed to stand up to computer analysis. The best known are two shots of a saucerlike object with a pointed top, taken in McMinnville, Oregon, in 1950. A photo of an identical disc was taken in Brazil in 1952, and a third in Rouen, France, in 1954.

By enhancing photos, computers can bring out details that aren't obvious to the eye. When photos of the strange lights that appeared over Belgium between 1989 and 1991 were computer-enhanced, they revealed a dark, triangular shape behind the lights. The downside of computers, of course, is that they can also be used to create fakes that are more convincing than ever.

In the 1960s the committee that produced the Condon Report analyzed fourteen photos of UFOs. They concluded that two pictures taken by a farmer and his wife in McMinnville, Oregon, in 1950 were genuine. This is one of them.

The UFO Enigma Museum in Roswell, New Mexico, depicts the craft that crashed nearby as a saucer shape, but some witnesses said it looked more like an airplane fuselage.

night sky, has been officially named the Extraterrestrial Highway. Roswell, New Mexico, is home to not one but two UFO museums. Elmwood, Wisconsin, where several dramatic close encounters took place in the 1970s, now holds an annual celebration called UFO Days.

There are more than a dozen active national UFO societies; two of them boast a hundred or more local chapters. Obviously there are still plenty of believers. When you took the quiz at the beginning of this book, you showed more or less where you stand on the subject. But don't make up your mind too quickly. We haven't looked at all the evidence yet.

PART TWO

Everything You Always Wanted to Know

about

UFOs

Like many things in life, UFOs tend to turn up when you're not looking for them. English photographer Jeremy Johnson was shooting a picture of the sky and didn't see the white object until the film was developed.

Classified
Information

The term *UFO* is a very broad one. It includes everything that's ever appeared in the skies and can't be
identified. But it doesn't make sense to assume that
there's a single, blanket explanation for all those strange lights and
objects.

J. Allen Hynek, the astronomer who investigated UFOs for the
Air Force's Project Blue Book, devised a method of classifying UFO
encounters. Most UFO investigators, or "ufologists," still use some
form of Hynek's classification system.

NOCTURNAL LIGHTS

The vast majority of sightings are actually nocturnal lights. As the
name indicates, these are bright lights of various colors, sometimes
flashing, that appear at night. Often they seem to dart about; at other
times they hover or move slowly across the sky. Most nocturnal lights
turn out not to be UFOs at all, but IFOs—*Identified* Flying Objects.
More than 80 percent of nocturnal-light sightings are really one of

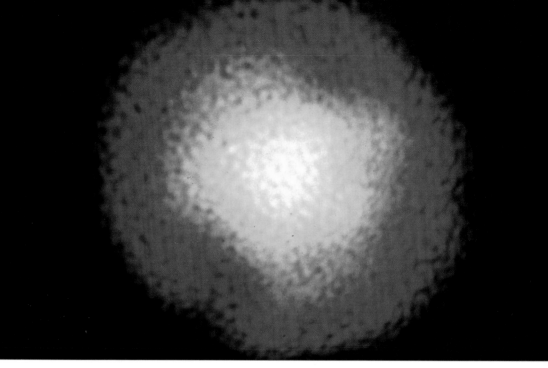

In 1984 a team of Scandinavian ufologists set up an array of scientific instruments in a remote valley in Norway.

four things: 1) stars and planets, 2) lighted advertising planes, 3) other aircraft, or 4) meteors and satellites entering the earth's atmosphere.

Sometimes, because of the earth's atmosphere, a bright star or planet can seem larger than it is, especially when it's near the horizon, and can appear to flash or to change color. Our own eye movements can make it seem to move. Venus is the most common culprit. During World War II the Navy's USS *Houston* fired 250 rounds in an attempt to shoot the planet down. An official at Detroit Metropolitan Airport

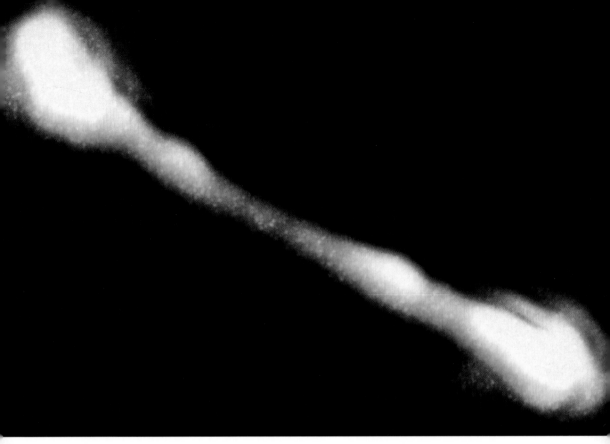

Over a period of just five weeks, the researchers recorded 188 sightings of nocturnal lights.

says, "Do you know how many times we've cleared Venus to land?"

When people see a row of lights, like those on an advertising plane, they tend to "connect the dots" and assume that's the shape of the object. So they report seeing everything from flying triangles to airborne doughnuts. One advertising plane in the 1960s caused a real uproar when it flew around with a lighted sign touting something called Unequaled Formula Oil (note the initials).

A group of British fishermen were terrified when a totally different sort of nocturnal light swooped over their heads. It turned out to be an owl that had eaten decayed fungi and was literally glowing in the dark!

DAYLIGHT DISCS

Despite the name, lots of shapes get lumped under the heading of daylight discs. These objects may look like circles, cigars, rectangles, mushrooms, or even straw hats. Daylight discs make up about 6 percent of UFO reports. But again, most are really IFOs. More than a third prove to be weather balloons reflecting sunlight. A fourth are ordinary aircraft, which can appear to take on odd shapes when they

This daylight disc was captured on film in New Mexico in 1957.

reflect the sun's glare. Meteors account for about 6 percent. Oddly, blimps are almost never reported as daylight UFOs.

RADAR-VISUALS

About 4 percent of UFO sightings have also shown up on radar. Most of these have turned out to be weather balloons.

These first three classifications—nocturnal lights, daylight discs, and radar-visuals—should probably be considered a whole separate category of UFOs. There's no real reason to assume that a far-off light or

a shiny shape automatically means an alien spacecraft when there are so many more obvious and credible explanations. Most good ufologists use a guiding principle called Occam's razor. This scientific rule of thumb says that when you're faced with a number of possible explanations for a phenomenon, you should pick the simplest one. Extraterrestrials may be the most *interesting* explanation of shapes in the sky, but they're not anyone's idea of the simplest.

CLOSE ENCOUNTERS

Now we get into the heart of the UFO enigma: close encounters. These are loosely defined as unexpected meetings in which the UFO comes within five hundred feet of the witness, close enough so that the witness can make out actual details.

There's still a lot of room for error, because an object can seem a lot closer than it really is, especially at night, which is when most sightings take place. Think about how close the moon can look, compared with its real distance, and you'll see how hard it is to estimate distance accurately.

Hynek grouped close encounters into three classifications called, rather unimaginatively, Close Encounters of the First Kind, the Second Kind, and the Third Kind. Some ufologists have proposed a fourth category.

Many shapes in the sky have a natural explanation. What seems to be a tripledecker UFO is more likely a circular cloud formation known as a lenticular cloud.

Close Encounters of the First Kind (CE1s)

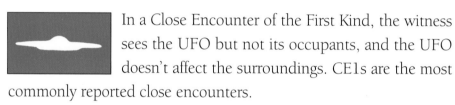 In a Close Encounter of the First Kind, the witness sees the UFO but not its occupants, and the UFO doesn't affect the surroundings. CE1s are the most commonly reported close encounters.

There are two broad explanations for CE1s: First, it could be that the witness is giving an *inaccurate* description of an *ordinary* object. Second, the witness might be giving an *accurate* description of an *extraordinary* object.

Inaccurate descriptions of ordinary objects head the list. Here again, stars, advertising planes, and other aircraft are the usual suspects, accounting for almost 70 percent of CE1s. People also mistake balloons, missiles, streetlights, and meteors for looming alien craft.

But there's a hard core of CE1s that defy easy explanation. Here are two of the best-known examples:

BEVERLY, Massachusetts. April 22, 1966. 9 P.M.

Through her bedroom window, eleven-year-old Nancy notices bright, flashing lights. She peers outside and sees a football-shaped object the size of a car hovering over the high school. Terrified, she runs to tell her mother, Claire. Sure that it's just an airplane, Claire takes two adult friends, Barbara and Brenda, and goes to check it out.

They discover two more oval objects circling around, as if playing tag. Brenda waves her arms playfully. To her surprise and alarm, one of the craft responds by gliding toward them. Barbara and Claire run away, but Brenda is frozen in place, screaming and covering her head with her hands, as the object hovers twenty feet above her. The others shout at her until she scrambles away.

Another witness calls the police, who show up joking, "Where's the airplane?" When one of the objects turns bright red and descends on the high school, the officers quit laughing and jump into their squad car. The objects take off and disappear. Three miles away, students at Gordon College watch a glowing orange oval pass silently a hundred feet overhead.

EXETER, New Hampshire. September 3, 1965. 2 A.M.

As Norman, a teenager, is hitchhiking on a road outside of town, five blindingly bright flashing red lights in a boomerang pattern appear over the rooftops. Silently they head in Norman's direction. He dives into a ditch. When the lights move off, he emerges, badly shaken, and catches a ride to the police station. A patrolman escorts him back to the scene.

The lighted object returns, too. "It lit up the entire field," the policeman later reported, "and two houses turned completely red. It stopped, hovered, and turned on a dime." The object "came so close I fell to the ground and started to draw my gun."

Norman yells, "Shoot it!" Instead the policeman herds him into the squad car and calls for backup. A second patrolman arrives in time to see the object retreat and disappear. At least sixty witnesses see similar objects in the area; some are picked up on radar and chased by Air Force planes.

Though the craft that Norman saw left no physical traces, it may have made its mark in another way. Two months later, on November 8, 1965, several witnesses in the northeastern United States reported seeing a red cigar shape hovering over power lines. The following day a pilot noticed a huge, brilliant red ball over an electrical power substation. At that same moment the electrical power grid failed, blacking out a fifth of the country.

The craft that turn up in CE1s come in all shapes and sizes (see chart), but most fit into one of six categories:

1) a glowing red or orange ball

2) a gray or white oval

3) a silvery cigar shape, sometimes with a row of windows. These craft are sometimes called "mother ships" because other shapes are seen leaving or entering them.

The classic saucer shape, displayed in triplicate in this 1960 photo from Italy, is just one of the many UFO shapes that have been reported by witnesses.

4) a "Saturn" shape—a metallic ball with a rim around it
5) the classic saucer—flat on the bottom, domed on top
6) a triangle or cone

Close Encounters of the Second Kind (CE2s)

 In CE2s, the object that's sighted affects the witness or the surroundings in some way. Naturally these are rarer than CE1s. Even so, one ufologist has recorded 4,400 cases of physical evidence ascribed to UFOs. CE2s are also harder to explain than CE1s, and usually involve fewer witnesses—though not always, as you'll see from the following account:

BRAZIL. July-September 1977.

Every evening for three months, strange craft of various sizes and shapes appear over a remote group of islands near the mouth of the Amazon River. They hover over houses and, from time to time, shoot out a beam of white light three inches in diameter.

Dozens of people are hit by the beam, and they're temporarily paralyzed. The local health center is flooded with patients who have been zapped and are complaining of dizziness, headaches, numbness, puncture marks, and burned skin. The villagers panic. Those who can, flee the islands. Those who can't, set off firecrackers and beat on pans in an attempt to scare away the objects. The Brazilian government sends in a team of doctors and scientists to investigate and to film the phenomenon.

Most CE2s don't last nearly this long, and they usually involve only a single witness, but a lot of these witnesses seem to have solid evidence and are very convincing.

FRANCE. November 2, 1968. 4 A.M.

A physician—call him Dr. X—is wakened by his one-year-old's crying. The boy is standing up in his crib, pointing to flashes of light outside. Dr. X steps onto the balcony. Two silvery discs about two hundred feet in diameter are sending beams of white light across the ground. The two discs merge into one object; it tilts, and the white beam catches the doctor in the chest. With a bang, the object disappears.

But its effects don't. Dr. X had been suffering from an old war wound, and three days before the sighting he had cut himself with an ax. Both injuries have suddenly healed completely. But the doctor feels weak and has a pain in his abdomen. Two weeks later a six-inch triangle of reddened skin, like a sunburn, appears on his stomach; an identical mark shows up on his young son. Though the marks fade, they reappear regularly for years afterward.

Not all the effects of CE2s are so dramatic. Some are merely depressions in the ground, presumably left by landing gear. A sixteen-year-old Kansas farm boy discovered a large circle in a field where he had seen a UFO take off. The soil in the ring glowed and shed water. Reports of UFOs routinely mention televisions going on the blink and car engines stalling, then starting up again once the UFO has left.

In December 1977, near Council Bluffs, Iowa, a glowing red object crashed and burned, igniting a grass fire. When police and firefighters arrived, they found a four-by-six-foot mass of molten metal, mostly iron, but with traces of nickel and chromium. The presence of these metals indicates that the object probably wasn't a meteorite.

In 1975 two students at the University of Bogotá in Colombia spotted a disc that seemed to be flying out of control. A stream of silvery liquid spouted from it and splashed onto the rain-drenched street. When the liquid cooled, the students picked up two small chunks of metal. Scientists analyzed it and found it was mostly aluminum and magnesium. The metal had been overheated, as if in an explosion.

UFOs have reportedly dropped even more mysterious things. In the 1960s a Wisconsin chicken farmer produced four pancakes left

In 1961 chicken farmer Joe Simonton claimed that four pieces of pancake-like bread were given to him by visiting aliens. His story earned him the nickname "Pancake Joe."

Crop Circles and Cut-up Cows

Some ufologists believe that UFOs are leaving behind more damage than just a few burn marks. Ever since the seventeenth century, mysterious flattened circles have been turning up in farmers' fields. The most recent rash began in 1973, when seven circles up to fourteen feet in diameter appeared overnight in a field of oats in Australia. Some blamed the mashed-down crops on rampaging kangaroos.

But beginning in 1980 similar circles started turning up in kangarooless England. Some have proved to be hoaxes, committed by pranksters who merely stomped the crops down in various patterns—including a smiley face. But it's relatively easy to tell the hoaxes from the real thing: The unexplained crop circles have sharply defined edges; they're simple circles, not complex patterns; and the stems of the crops aren't just trampled down, they're swirled around and interwoven.

Because the circles often occur in UFO-haunted areas, some investigators suspect them of being "saucer nests," where alien craft have set down, or even of being mysterious messages from outer space. But there's a more down-to-earth theory. The crop circles may be formed by something called a plasma vortex, a spinning column of air, like a mini tornado, that can carry an electrical charge.

A widespread wave of animal mutilations has also been blamed on aliens. The first known case was recorded during the "mystery airship" scare of 1897. A Kansas farmer saw one of his heifers being towed off by an airship; the next day the cow's head, legs, and hide were discovered by a neighbor four miles away.

The current wave started in 1967, when a horse called Snippy was found dead on a ranch near Alamosa, Colorado. Its chest organs had been removed with surgical precision, and its blood drained. Bushes nearby were flattened, and there were strange holes and burn marks on the ground. Strangest of all, poor Snippy's hoofprints ended one hundred feet from where his carcass lay, as if he'd been lifted and carried somehow, then dropped to the ground. Since then there have been several thousand reports of similar mutilations, mostly of cattle, from all over the world. No one has come up with a simple explanation yet.

These crop circles were discovered in the English countryside in 1990.

behind, he said, by an alien craft. When tested, they proved to be quite ordinary, made of three or four different grains.

A substance called "angel hair" is often reported dropping from the sky during UFO sightings. Unfortunately it dissolves when touched, which makes it tough to examine. The few samples that have survived have turned out to be nothing more than webs of the balloon spider, drifting on the wind.

Close Encounters of the Third Kind (CE3s)

 The debate over CE2s is mild compared to the one surrounding CE3s. In these cases, witnesses see or even interact with extraterrestrial beings. Throughout most of the history of UFOs, these have been the rarest cases of all. But ever since the 1970s they've been on the rise, especially those that involve people being abducted by aliens. Some ufologists now suggest that there should be a new category, CE4, to cover abductions because, as you'll see, they do seem to be a whole separate phenomenon.

There are at least three thousand recorded CE3s. The most celebrated is referred to as the "Roswell incident." Because it happened fifty years ago, it's hard to sort out fact from myth. But it wouldn't be fair to write about UFOs without recounting the story in some depth:

FOSTER RANCH, New Mexico. June 14, 1947.
Ten days before Kenneth Arnold's sighting of objects that flew like "saucers" over Washington State, the foreman on a sheep ranch near Corona, New Mexico, discovers a field full of strange, shiny

material. He notifies Major Jesse Marcel, the intelligence officer at nearby Roswell Army Air Field. Marcel checks it out and brings home a truckload of debris that includes sticks of light brown "plastic" and pieces of foil-like material printed with pink and purple "hieroglyphics."

On July 8 the public information officer at the air base makes a startling statement to the press: "The many rumors regarding the flying disc became a reality yesterday when the Intelligence Office was fortunate enough to gain possession of a disc. . . ."

The story goes out to radio stations and newspapers across the country. The air base is flooded with calls from reporters. But three hours later the Air Force contradicts itself with a second news release, which states that the "flying saucer" is, in fact, nothing more than a crashed weather balloon.

This could have been the end of the matter. Certainly the Air Force seemed to hope it would be. But thirty years later Jesse Marcel, the former intelligence officer, brought it back to life by revealing what he'd seen. Ufologists investigated and turned up more witnesses. Some of them had seen more than just shiny debris; they'd seen bodies. According to one witness, the aliens were "smaller than a normal man—about four feet—and had much larger heads than us, with slanted eyes."

A mortician from the town of Roswell reported that on July 9 or 10, 1947, he got a call from the army airfield, asking questions about how to handle dead bodies. The following day a friend of the mortician's, who was a nurse at the air base, came to see him. She was

The Air Force stated in 1947 that what crashed near Roswell, New Mexico, was a weather balloon and displayed the debris to prove it. But some researchers believed the materials the Air Force displayed weren't the same as those recovered from the crash site.

very upset. She said she had seen three alien bodies brought in. She described them in detail and even made sketches of their strange hands and faces.

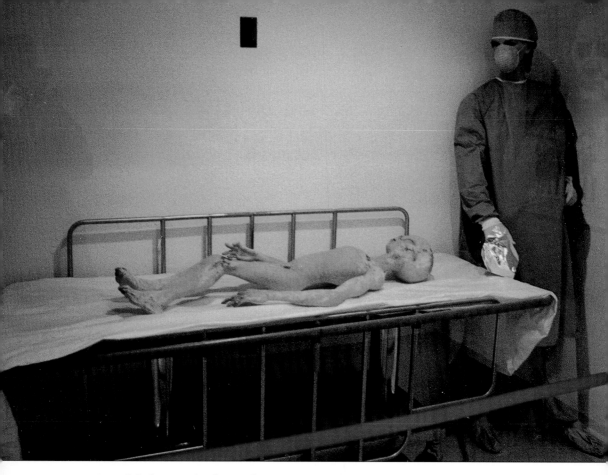

A model alien on display at the International UFO Museum and Research Center in Roswell, New Mexico. The museum exhibit re-creates an alleged autopsy of one of the alien bodies believed to have been retrieved by the Air Force after a UFO crash.

In 1989 and 1990 new witnesses came forward to reveal that there had been a second crash, 150 miles west of the first. It, too, involved alien astronauts, and apparently one was found alive and moving.

In 1997, as the fiftieth anniversary of the Roswell incident approached, there was a whole new flurry of speculation about what had crashed in New Mexico. An article in *Popular Mechanics* magazine concluded that there really was a crashed disc and that it was piloted not by extraterrestrials but by Japanese airmen. That accounts, the article stated, for the small stature and "Oriental features" of the so-called aliens.

The Air Force stuck to its original story, with a few new variations. The debris, the officials now said, was the remains not of a weather balloon but of an observation balloon developed by the top-secret Project Mogul to keep an eye on nuclear testing in the Soviet Union. And what about the alien bodies? They were dummies, dropped from the Project Mogul balloon to study what happened when they hit the ground. The dummies were described as being three and a half feet to four feet tall, with no ears or hair. How one of the dummies managed to sit up and move around is left unexplained.

This official explanation seems plausible enough, except that it's contradicted by so many witnesses, some of them former high-ranking military officers. Philip J. Corso, a retired Army intelligence officer, insists that he saw the bodies, floating in tanks of liquid. What's more, he claims that the military studied the debris from the crashed craft, then passed the knowledge on to large American corporations who used it to develop new technologies such as fiber optics and integrated circuits.

A retired colonel stationed at Roswell during the incident says that the "weather balloon story was a complete fabrication" and that the wreckage was flown to Wright Field in Ohio (now Wright-Patterson Air Force Base). Several other witnesses have reported seeing the remains of the alien bodies there. A former general who was at Wright Field in 1947 flatly states that what took place at Roswell "was the recovery of a craft from space."

The Roswell incident is just the most publicized CE3. There are plenty of others that are less well known but even better documented.

PAPUA, New Guinea. June 26, 1959. 6:45 P.M.

Anglican missionary Father William Gill and thirty of his parishioners stare at a bright, sparkling object descending from the sky. Four figures appear on a sort of deck atop the object; they are, Father William later reports, "occasionally bending over and raising their arms as though adjusting or setting up something." Heavy rain ends the encounter, but the next evening the UFO is back; again the figures are on deck. Father William waves at them. The aliens wave back. When he signals the craft with a flashlight, it responds by rocking back and forth.

KELLY, Kentucky. August 21, 1955.

Twenty-one-year-old Billy Ray Taylor is visiting a friend's farm when he sees a flying saucer plunge into a nearby gully. Half an hour later, a strange form approaches the farmhouse. It is a three-foot-tall, glowing figure with large, pointed ears on an egg-shaped bald head. Long, skinny arms dangle at its sides. Frightened, Billy Ray and his friend grab guns and fire at the figure. It does a somersault but seems unharmed. Two other aliens turn up and peer into the windows; they, too, seem unfazed by the gunfire. There are eleven witnesses to the incident, and the details of their accounts agree.

The descriptions given by the Roswell witnesses and those in

Convincing photos of alien astronauts are almost nonexistent. This one, taken near Mexico City in the 1950s, is a fake. The "extraterrestrial" is probably a monkey with its fur shaved off.

Kentucky fit the usual image of alien astronauts. But extraterrestrials come in as many shapes and sizes as the UFOs themselves. There are reports of ten-foot-tall giants and of elves, of hairy dwarfs and of robots, sometimes even of very humanlike figures. One ufologist points out that if these really are extraterrestrials, they must come from half a dozen different planets. Another expert notes that the aliens are seldom seen wearing space suits or breathing apparatus. How are they able to breathe our atmosphere?

Close Encounters of the Fourth Kind (CE4s)

For thousands of years there have been reports of people being taken for rides into the heavens. One story involved a Jesuit priest named Athanasius Kircher. In 1656 he wrote that two "angels" took him on a tour of the sun and the planets. But alien abductions, in which subjects are taken aboard a spaceship against their will, seem to be a modern phenomenon, and a very controversial one. Unlike CE1s, CE2s, and some CE3s, there's a notable lack of supporting witnesses. In almost all CE4s, no one sees the incident except the person being abducted.

To further complicate matters, most of the time the "abductees" don't consciously remember their experiences. They often have emotional problems, nightmares, or a "lost" period of time they can't account for. It isn't until they're put under hypnosis that they can recount the whole abduction experience. The details, at least in American abduction reports, are strikingly similar. There is usually a blinding white light, a feeling of being paralyzed, then a memory of being "floated" into a craft and examined in a hospital-like room by humanoid creatures.

As in CE3s, descriptions of the aliens vary, but the most commonly described being is three or four feet tall, with spindly arms and legs and a large head. The nose and mouth are hardly noticeable, but the eyes are huge and black.

The fact that abduction stories are so much alike seems to suggest that we're dealing with a real experience, not an imagined one. But an experiment conducted at California State University in 1977 raises serious doubts. Eight volunteers were hypnotized and asked, without any coaching, to invent a fictitious abduction story. The details they came up with were surprisingly close to those in accounts of "real" abductions. Apparently we've been exposed to so much information about UFOs, in newspapers and books, in movies and on TV, that we all have a built-in idea of what spaceships and aliens and even abductions are "supposed" to look like.

But there may be more to it than that. Scientists know that when the area of the brain called the temporal lobe is disturbed, either by drugs or by an electrical current, the brain creates an array of real-seeming feelings and images—hallucinations, in other words. These feelings and images turn up not only in abduction stories, but also in stories of near-death experiences and out-of-body experiences. They include a floating sensation, bright lights, voices, distorted human and animal figures, landscapes, passing through a tunnel, and seeing events from the person's life.

Could seeing a UFO somehow affect the temporal lobe of the brain and trigger hallucinations like these? Certainly there are plenty of electrical effects linked to UFOs: TV interference, stalled cars, hair standing on end, temporary paralysis, buzzing sounds, burned areas.

These effects are so common, in fact, that some scientists think UFOs may be pure electrical energy. They point to an unusual form of lightning called ball lightning as the source. Other scientists think that electrical "coronas" given off by power lines are responsible.

These energy sources may account for some UFOs. But the most convincing theory about the electrical nature of UFOs involves something called earth lights. Though earth lights have been around at

Some scientists believe that ball lightning is responsible for a lot of UFO sightings, but this form of lightning is rare and usually lasts only a few seconds.

least as long as people have, we don't know much about them. We do know that they tend to appear where there are active volcanoes or earthquake faults. They seem to emerge from the ground or from water; usually they disappear quickly, but they can hover in the air at a height of thousands of feet and can even "fly" for some distance. They seem to be a prime candidate for unidentified nocturnal lights, and maybe for unidentified daylight discs, too, since they can look metallic in daylight. This theory seems even more likely when you consider that the areas where UFOs are sighted most often are also areas where volcanoes and major earthquake faults are located.

But just as there's no reason to assume that all UFOs are from outer space, there's no reason to call them all earth lights, either. Several noted ufologists think that UFOs are a paranormal phenomenon, that they come from some other dimension that exists alongside ours but that we can't ordinarily see. One writer calls this invisible dimension the "superspectrum." These ufologists believe that many other unexplained phenomena, such as ghosts, goblins, fairies, Bigfoot, and the Loch Ness monster, also belong to this other dimension and that they somehow "break through" into our world from time to time.

It's an intriguing idea. But again, it doesn't necessarily account for all UFOs. Some could well be experimental aircraft being developed by our military. And we certainly can't rule out the possibility that some of them really may be visitors from outer space. Astronomer Carl Sagan said the odds are that there are at least ten other inhabited planets within one thousand light years of ours, and some undoubtedly have technology that's far ahead of ours.

Pseudo-saucers

In 1655, when he was thirteen, the famed Isaac Newton created a sensation by flying a kite with a lantern attached to it over his home town in Lincolnshire, England. He probably wasn't the first to construct his own UFO, and he certainly wasn't the last.

During the airship craze of 1897 a man in Waterloo, Iowa, built a bogus airship of lumber and canvas and attracted a crowd of five thousand. Nearly a century later two boys built a crude sheet-metal saucer, equipped it with battery-powered flashing lights, and placed it in the middle of a country road. They fooled several startled drivers, but eventually the police arrived, with guns drawn, and kicked the saucer off the road in disgust.

Not all human-made UFOs were meant to be hoaxes. Several inventors have tried to build workable saucer-type aircraft. After World War II the Navy developed a circular craft called the Flying Flapjack; it never got off the ground. In the 1950s the Air Force built and tested a jet-propelled saucer called the Avrocar, but it proved too unstable to fly well.

In 1962 a French inventor came up with a disc that was held aloft by two large horizontal propellers; he claimed the craft would go one hundred miles per hour, but he couldn't prove it. In 1986 the Moller 200X, a one-passenger saucer with eight small propellers, managed to fly at a height of thirty-five feet.

Obviously these experimental craft couldn't have been responsible for more than a few UFO sightings. But it's almost certain that some of the new aircraft under development by the Air Force have been mistaken for alien ships. When seen straight on, the B2 Stealth bomber, first flown in 1989, looks remarkably like the classic domed saucer.

The B-2 Stealth bomber

It is hard to imagine, though, why aliens would come all that way and then not even bother to stop and chat, eat at McDonald's, buy a few souvenirs, or spend a day at Disneyworld.

Where to See UFOs

Areas where UFOs are regularly sighted are called windows. There are several major windows in the United States. Chances are you live near one. If you can visit one, and if you're patient, you may well get a look at a UFO. Here are some good bets:

1) The Yakima Indian Reservation in Washington State, south of Mount Rainier. Here's where Kenneth Arnold spotted those objects the press called flying saucers. Since then, there have been hundreds of reports of UFOs in this area.

2) The area around Niagara Falls. There's a lot of helicopter traffic around the falls themselves, so the best place to sky-watch is in the rural area along the south shore of Lake Ontario.

3) The Texas Triangle. The points of the triangle are Lubbock, Texas; Alpine, Texas; and Albuquerque, New Mexico. Half a dozen of the most significant UFO encounters happened here, including the Roswell incident. The area east of Marfa, Texas, boasts the "Marfa lights," which have been dancing in the skies for centuries.

4) The Gulf Strip. A one-hundred-mile stretch of coast along

the Gulf of Mexico from Biloxi, Mississippi, to Pensacola, Florida. The Pensacola Bay Bridge is a good place to sky-watch.

5) The New Madrid area of southeast Missouri, the site of a major quake in the 1800s. After mysterious balls of light were seen here in 1973, a physics professor set up Project Identification. Over a period of seven years, his team logged 178 unidentified objects. Some of them seemed to respond to radio messages and visual signals.

6) Nevada Highway 375, north of Las Vegas. It's been named the

A reliable spot for viewing nocturnal lights is on U.S. Highway 90 between Marfa and Alpine, Texas. Some scholars suggest that the "Marfa lights" are just distorted beams from car headlights, but experiments have disproved that theory.

Extraterrestrial Highway because of the many nocturnal lights and saucer shapes spotted along it. One light turns up so regularly that it's nicknamed Old Faithful. To the south lies Area 51, a remote part of Nellis Air Force Base. Some say the Air Force is testing futuristic aircraft there. Others say it's an alien landing site.

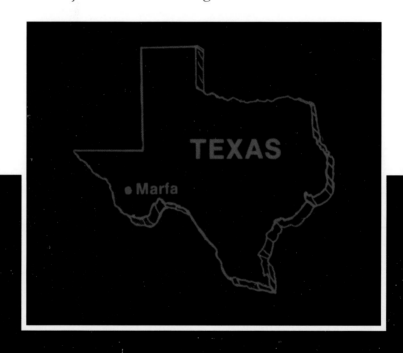

What to Do If
You See a UFO

Nocturnal lights and daylight discs are pretty common, especially in the areas called windows, and probably aren't worth reporting to anybody except your family and friends. But suppose you're lucky enough to have a close encounter. What should you do?

First, try to get other witnesses. Second, take photos if you can. Third, take notes, paying special attention to the following:

1) How big is the UFO? Compare it to other objects in the sky, like the sun or the moon.

2) What shape is it?

3) What features do you notice? Blinking lights? Windows? Antennae? Landing gear? A dome?

4) Where is it in the sky? How many degrees above the horizon?

5) In what direction is it moving?

6) How long is it visible? How does it disappear?

7) What is the weather like?

8) If there are animals around, how do they react?

Where do you report your sighting? Not to a newspaper; that can get you unwanted publicity. The police aren't likely to be very interested. But civilian UFO groups will be. There's a list of organizations you can contact at the back of this book.

If the unthinkable happens, and you find yourself face to face with alien astronauts, *then* what do you do? *The Book of Survival* (Harper & Row, 1967) recommends that you 1) avoid rapid, forceful movements; 2) make no shrill sounds; 3) breathe quietly (if you can!); and 4) avoid looking at the aliens in a direct, menacing way.

In 1994 *Omni* magazine asked well-known scientists, writers, and public figures what they would say if they met an extraterrestrial. Here are some of their responses:

Actor Bruce Campbell: "What took you so long?"

Author Douglas Rushkoff: "Please pardon our appearance while we remodel."

Playwright Arthur Miller: "Go back! You can get killed here!"

Philadelphia Mayor Edward G. Rendell: "I'd ask them if they had  a cure for AIDS, unemployment, crime, drugs, hopelessness, and the breakdown of the family."

Writer Harlan Ellison: "Help us. We are very young, and we want to know."

Humorist Dave Barry: "Do you guys have cable?"

CNN anchor Bernard Shaw: "I would run!"

Glossary

abduction: A kidnapping; taking a person away secretly, often by force.

aborigines: The earliest inhabitants of a country.

ball lightning: A rare type of lightning in the form of a sphere, up to forty inches in diameter, which usually disappears within a few seconds, sometimes with a bang.

balloon spider: A kind of spider that travels to new locations by spinning a web that floats through the air.

Buck Rogers: The hero of a 1930s science fiction comic strip and subsequent movie serials.

Churchill, Winston: Prime minister of Great Britain, 1940–1945, 1951–1955.

dirigible: Also known as an airship. A lighter-than-air craft that consists of a gas-filled balloon with a passenger compartment underneath.

Gallup poll: A survey of public opinion on some issue, using market research methods developed by statistician George H. Gallup.

Gemini IV: The second piloted mission in the Gemini program of space flights. The *Gemini IV* spacecraft orbited the earth for four days.

hieroglyphics: An early form of writing, using mainly pictorial symbols; also, any written message that's hard to decipher.

Hiroshima: A Japanese city destroyed by the first atomic bomb on August 6, 1945.

Nazis: Members of the National Socialist German Workers Party, founded by Adolf Hitler and in power in Germany during World War II.

near-death experience: A series of images that occur to one out of three people who physically die, or nearly die, and are resuscitated. Case histories are explored in the book *Life After Life,* by Raymond Moody.

Newton, Isaac (1642–1727): An English scientific genius who first formulated the laws of motion and gravity.

out-of-body experience: The feeling that you're seeing yourself and your body from some point outside the body, as if the soul or mind has left the body and is acting separately, sometimes traveling to other places.

paranormal: A term used to describe a wide variety of phenomena that are outside the bounds of everyday experience. Examples are extrasensory perception (ESP), ghosts, telepathy, prophecy, magic—the sorts of things once called "supernatural."

Pearl Harbor: The surprise Japanese air attack on the U.S. forces based at Pearl Harbor, Hawaii, on December 7, 1941; the attack drew the United States into World War II.

seismograph: An instrument that measures and records the vibrations from earthquakes.

skeptic: A person who doubts something that is claimed to be true.

temporal lobe: The area at the base of the brain that controls hearing, balance, memory, and smell.

weather balloon: A lightweight balloon made of thin, tough materials and equipped with instruments that collect weather information in the upper atmosphere.

To Learn More about UFOs

BOOKS-NONFICTION

Deem, James M. *How to Catch a Flying Saucer.* Boston: Houghton Mifflin, 1991. A levelheaded account of UFOs, full of useful information and lively drawings; includes a section on how to become a ufologist. Very readable.

Larsen, Sherman J. *Close Encounters: A Factual Report on UFOs.* Milwaukee: Raintree, 1978. A simple overview of the UFO phenomenon. Color photos.

Randles, Jenny, and Peter A. Hough. *World's Best "True" UFO Stories.* New York: Sterling, 1994. Brief, dramatic accounts of some of the more interesting and well-known close encounters.

BOOKS-FICTION

DeWeese, Gene. *Major Corby and the Unidentified Flapping Object.* Garden City, N. Y.: Doubleday, 1979. Tale of a fourteen-year-old boy who encounters a glowing ball, a scout from an alien ship.

McMurtry, Ken. *A History Mystery: The Mystery of the Roswell UFO.* New York: Avon, 1992.

MUSEUMS

International UFO Museum and Research Center, 400-402 North Main, Roswell, N.M. 88202. Displays, research materials, gift shop.

UFO Enigma Museum, 6108 South Main, Roswell, N.M. 88202. Features a large display dealing with the Roswell incident.

ORGANIZATIONS

Amalgamated Flying Saucer Clubs of America, P.O. Box 39, Yucca Valley, Calif. 92286. Contact them to find out if there's a UFO club near you. Publishes a quarterly newsletter, *Flying Saucers International*.

J. Allen Hynek Center for UFO Studies, 2457 W. Peterson Ave., Suite 6, Chicago, Ill. 60659. Collects reports of UFO sightings, publishes a bimonthly magazine, *International UFO Reporter*.

Mutual UFO Network, 103 Oldtowne Road, Seguin, Texas 78155-4099. Has fifty state groups and sixty local groups. Holds a convention each July. Publishes a monthly magazine, *MUFON UFO Journal*.

UFO Information Retrieval Center, 3131 West Cochise Drive, #158, Phoenix, Ariz. 85051-9501. Offers services for children and students; speakers.

VIDEOS

UFO: The Unsolved Mystery. LBS Extraterrestrial Inc., 1989. Amateurish, but features brief interviews with noted ufologists.

Index

Page numbers for illustrations are in bold face.

INDEX

Notes

Quotes in this book are from the following sources:

Page 19 "This 'flying saucer' situation": *Crash at Corona: The U.S. Military Retrieval and Cover-up of a UFO,* by Stanton T. Friedman and Don Berliner (New York: Paragon House, 1992), p. 21.

Page 20 "They flew like a saucer would": *UFOs and How to See Them,* by Jenny Randles (New York: Sterling, 1992), p. 16.

Page 23 "If I saw a ten-story building": The *UFO Controversy in America,* by David Michael Jacobs (Bloomington: Indiana University Press, 1975), p. 38.

Page 23 "from some extraterrestrial source": *UFOs and Related Subjects: An Annotated Bibliography,* by Lynn E. Catoe (Detroit: Gale, 1978), p. 213.

Page 39 "Do you know how many times": *The UFO Handbook: A Guide to Investigating, Evaluating, and Reporting UFO Sightings,* by Allan Hendry (Garden City, N. Y.: Doubleday, 1979), p. 27.

Page 45 "It lit up the entire field": *The Hynek UFO Report,* by Dr. J. Allen Hynek (New York: Dell, 1977), p. 164.

Page 56 "The many rumors": *Crash at Corona*, p. xiii.

Page 56 "smaller than a normal man": *Crash at Corona*, p. 128.

Page 59 "weather balloon story": *UFO Retrievals: The Recovery of Alien Spacecraft,* by Jenny Randles (London: Blandford, 1995), p. 45.

Page 60 "was the recovery of a craft": *Alien Encounters,* by editors of Time-Life Books (Alexandria, Va.: Time-Life, 1992), p. 85.

Page 60 "occasionally bending over": *The Hynek UFO Report*, p. 220.

About the Author

Gary L. Blackwood is a novelist and playwright who specializes in historical topics. His interest in the Unexplained goes back to his childhood, when he heard his father tell a story about meeting a ghost on a lonely country road.

Though he has yet to see a single UFO or ghost, a glimpse of the future or a past life, the author is keeping his eyes and his mind open. Gary lives in Missouri with his wife and two children.